C000182579

LATE LOVE POEMS

STEVE GRIFFITHS

INDEPENDENT INNOVATIVE INTERNATIONAL

Published by Cinnamon Press
Meirion House
Tanygrisiau
Blaenau Ffestiniog
Gwynedd, LL41 3SU
www.cinnamonpress.com
The right of steve Griffiths to be identified as author of this work has been asserted by him in accordance with the Copyright, Designs and Patent Act, 1988. Copyright © 2015 Steve Griffiths ISBN:978-1-910836-04-0.
British Library Cataloguing in Publication Data. A CIP record for this book can be obtained from the British Library.
All rights reserved. No part of this publication may be reproduced, stored in a retrieval system, or transmitted in any form or by any means, electronic, mechanical, photocopying, recording or otherwise without the prior written permission of the publishers. This book may not be lent, hired out, resold or otherwise disposed of by way of trade in any form of binding or cover other than that in which it is published, without the prior consent of the publishers.
Designed and typeset in Palatino by Cinnamon Press. Printed in Poland.
Cover design by Jan Fortune from an original painting 'Lit' by Carlos Torres © Carlos Torres (2015).
Cinnamon Press is represented in the UK by Inpress Ltd www.inpressbooks.co.uk and in Wales by the Welsh Books Council www.cllc.org.uk. The publisher acknowledges the support of the Welsh Books Council.

Acknowledgements

A number of these poems appeared in *Poetry Wales*. Others appeared in The Rialto, The Same (USA), The Wenlock Poetry Festival Anthology, and the pamphlet 'Landing', published by Rack Press (2008). Several of the poems have been read on BBC Radio Shropshire and BBC Radio Wales' *The Arts Show*.

Thirty-five of the poems feature in the Late Love Poems Film Project, shown in performance by Steve Griffiths week by week on YouTube between July 2015 and January 2016. The films can be accessed through www.latelovepoems.com.

Thanks are due:

To Arts Council England and the National Lottery for funding the films.

To the project's Social Media Partners: Filmpoem, Dylan Thomas Centre, Shropshire Libraries, Planet Magazine, Orkney Library, Wales Arts Review, Ludlow Fringe, Wenlock Books, and Poetry Wales, for helping to develop the audience for the films and for their invaluable support.

To others who have given valuable support in developing the audience for the films: The Poetry Society, Literature Wales, Poetry London, Bare Fiction, Gransnet, Hereford Library, and BBC Radio Shropshire.

To Eamon Bourke of park6productions, his film work the cornerstone of the project, for his framing and editing, his generosity, his coaxing of performance, his composure, his enthusiasm, his love for the text, his commitment to making a challenging creative partnership work, his feeling for the rhythm of a short film, and his friendship.

To Liz Hyder, the project's Social Media and PR Lead, for her patience, professionalism, encouragement and enthusiasm as I creaked towards an understanding of Twitter and Facebook; and her confident and persuasive navigation of a whole world out there.

To Jules May, who supported Eamon Bourke with sound, camera assist and photography; a calm and warm man to work with.

To Ivan 'Ogmios' Owen and John Hywel for the transformative powers of their music.

To Robert Minhinnick, Jean Atkin and Paul Greatorex, and Carlos Torres for their steadfast friendship, and to Carlos for yet another extraordinary gift of a book cover.

To Jan Fortune, for sticking with a formerly very retiring poet.

To Wendy, who in addition to the many qualities celebrated herein has put up with the lengthy palaver of my film project and mostly remembered what gave rise to it - and reminded me when I forgot.   For her critical acumen in response to some poems and other things that didn't work, and her warm enthusiasm for some that did.   For being the hand I hold.

Contents

Reaching for plums	9
Touch and vision	10
Turning his back to her	11
Backstroke	12
Gastronomy	13
Imprint	14
I find you	15
Explain this to me	16
The same place	17
Anniversary	18
A Pair for Bodies	19
Second person	20
Virtually	21
Echo	22
When I lost you the second time	23
Heart	24
Missing double maths with you	26
A compelling case	27
World	30
Padding back from a wintry bathroom	31
Listen	32
Discoveries	33
The spotted leaves of some marsh orchids	36
In Sickness	38
River	40
To arrive at breakfast...	41
The mistake	42
Gathering	44
The Harrowing of the Squamous Cell Carcinoma	45
January	48
Thursday, after making love	49
Wedding video	50
Five years of this illness pass	51

To Wendy

The apple tree said,
I will remain unexpected
for a lifetime

Cave	52
Life with you	53
Being strong	54
Pain	55
Walking out again	56
Spring	57
Lying on the mountainside	58

Late Love Poems

Reaching for plums

In summer rain inside a plum tree
we two stretch and climb and reach
to loosen all the ripe fruits that we can.
In your hooded anorak, the moment's
concentrated in the oval of your face —
if mine's the same, our mouths and eyes
are seeking out, our faces smoothed
and soaked and shining as the plums —
our anoraks so out of fashion
they're no longer waterproof.
The rain drums at the plastic on our heads.
Our first kiss damp, but then the burning spreads.
The fashions wash against you and recede.
You came round again like one of those, and stayed.

Touch and vision

At the summit, with your calves still
trembling a little from the climb,
your long back leans into my chest,
the small of it arcing away
from my belly and returning to me
in the very fitting curve of your bum;
and our faces burning
with the moment and the cold air
and touching, we look out together
at a field on the other side of the valley
through drifting screens of cloud,
the view muffled like our soundlessness
in the drizzle, then less pallid
fleetingly, and there's a radiant square
of green that has something of the gold
from a sudden directed column of light
on fields of stubble beside it

and the sun pours onto the mist below us
for all the world as if we were flying,
our bodies looking out for each other.

Turning his back to her

What I celebrate
is how you curve about
my turn away —
my facing you acknowledged
in its fullness, how the emissaries multiply
through the long lines of contact,
belly, pelvis, thigh,
ribs, shoulder, brow, and eye —
then how your affirming curiosity
has found a greater surface area
through the back
of my old green dreaming teeshirt —
how through it, with an unexpected
leap in capacity, the love leaks out.

Backstroke

The Buddha's eyes are squinting
at the sun across the field.
He seems contented in his alcove
and he smiles down as you strike
away from him across his pool.
The camera's caught the spray
illuminated, falling back, each drop
your consequence, as with your wake
attached, you pull away.
All motion, you create a symmetry
against the stillness resting in the wall.
At the end your white arm stretches to,
I look out from the shadow of a tree.
Your blonde hair's dark beneath the childish blue,
your parting cleaves a liquid paradox
of line and surface; as your movement
shimmers, flickers, thrashes, undulates,
your eyes fixed on the sky and what's ahead,
your fingertip just skims the apex
of my living geometry of deep content.

Gastronomy

The grape kiss,
its fleshy tang and sweet uplift;
the marmelade kiss,
the humble kiss of buttered toast
on the tongue
that prematurely
led upstairs again;
the white wine kiss
and its inexplicable
acceleration to cognac;
but the kiss I remember most
with its golden, resonant succulence
is the roast parsnip kiss.

Imprint

The sound of you
undressing in the dark.
You slip out
of one human form —
imprints left
on the hidden air —
entering another.

I find you

Cumulo-nimbus:
its dark attentive
resonance;
lightning in bolts
that roll slowly
up and down the vertebrae.
Then out the other side,
that clear light.
Humming residue
in the brain.
Co-ordination shot.
I find you again.

Explain this to me

In the morning, our glasses
were tangled in the same case

The same place

The storm binges on after hours
through darkened isobars.
A tornado in Kensal Rise,
which rises as it must.
The wind is chest-thumpingly high
round the house on the hilltop
where you live, bathed in leaves
in their changing ways.
My love for the gale's deep-rooted
but this bracing howl's a test.
The timbers strain, the house slips
anchor, spins, slowly at first,
then I hear you chuckle under the quilt,
and I'm certain we belong within the same
point on the map, in the same
rumpled bed, on the same swirl of contours.

Anniversary

Together
we found a small apple tree
in the wrong place,
on the last ridge of dune
that faced mountains
over a sheltered sea.

It was in blossom,
surrounded by sand
that shifted through marram.
The apple tree said,
I will remain unexpected
for a lifetime.

A Pair for Bodies

1

Our skins are so different together
under the bower of the quilt,
the suffused light on them
bringing them out:
what you call the yellow of yours,
what I call golden, with a foolish
eagerness that can't belie my years;
and mine, that hairy Celtic
butcher's white (to be particular,
an off-white that's informed by pink):
purity, surprise and gratitude,
these I find in the mix
of my skin's colour
only next to yours
under the tent.
What's more, sometimes
you scorch my bristles,
make me think.

2

The temple of the body:
both ours flaking,
some structural damage.
You don't get that presence,
the colour of the sun on warm,
warm stone in the late afternoon
without inspiration from the lives
that passed by it,
leaned on it.
Worth visiting.
But then we find
that due to the pressures of the attraction,
the wearing and tearing,
it's closed for a month,
for restoration.

Second person

You know how in different bathrooms,
don't you, the daylight comes
from the right or the left
as you face the mirror.
On weekends away, repeatedly
you see with a start
white hairs you didn't see before
that stretch out at right angles
from your beard, your ear
even: old man's horizontal tendrils,
an affront to dignity.
How long have they been doing that?
Who's this old man
who needs someone tender
to point out the mocking outcrops?

Virtually

We were searching for clinical guidelines
from remote workstations:
you scrolling down for depression,
I for the cost-effectiveness of physical activity,
in the same website together, unaware
and separated by a river and a city
and a concentration.
But there's no dividing membrane
in the virtual world or the insistent kind
that will keep us apart,
and now you mention it I swear
I could see the outline of your hand,
your face, and then the imprints of our bodies
pressed upon the web.
They did at least maintain some opacity.
And were gone, carried away as you swam
with your easy stroke
and your personal mouse
through the airwaves.
There's a residual crackling.
Something momentary, unrealised,
that would power a small town.

Echo

You were the one I called.
You comforted me
as I paced a kitchen
more relationships ago
than I rightly remember.
I think I howled
with grief and incomprehension,
though it was my doing.
Not long after it was your turn.
I remember the swell of abandon,
not a hint of a future landscape
of homecoming, not a hint
of a promise that remained
unseen till it was too late,
like a view of the garden
from your window
while my attention was diverted.
Later, much more
than my fingers were burned.
It wasn't a question of a script
I hadn't learned.
It was a love defeated
and confused and young.

I still might not forgive
those self-important lyrics
that hung around too long.
But my immaturity
was the one I lived:
it was mine then
as you were not.
Thirty-six years
echo with incredulity
that I recovered you,
that we are ready
as we were not.

When I lost you the second time

The dew in your lush borderland.
Towpaths overgrown.
The canals, the rivers, the seas
I couldn't swim.

Heart

Why do I always remember
my mother's words
from her one encounter with you
that if I fell down the toilet
I'd come up with a bunch of violets?
I was getting over
the last cohabitation,
off and on the vexing bicycle
of love: it was the falling off
that wasn't any easier
but here was something different
she thought she saw
that made her throat catch for me —
this I knew she meant,
barbed and wise
and hopeful for a moment,
if I fell in love with you.
You were a smart bunch of violets.
I wasn't yet connected up.
Smitten as I was, I bothered you
as you drove, just out of your teens,
tall and still coltish as you sat
on your dignity at the wheel
of your grey little A35,
I not knowing how to put
my overflowing want.
Not driving yet myself,
I never stood a chance
and then a common strand
through all the rich young detail
of the women who came after you,
all that I didn't cotton on to,
was the wanting to catch up
with something vanished up ahead
that others had — a hurtful
dislocation, heartless in effect,

I realise as I celebrate
a perceptible beat,
an irregular, soft,
insistent uplift.

Missing double maths with you

We lay on a beach
an imaginary forty years ago.
It was not warm in your dream.
I was naked, you were in pyjamas.
It was a Monday afternoon
and you were missing double maths.
I was in several dramas.
You covered me with my dressing gown.
Just out of reach.

A compelling case

I'm moving in with you

so the white wine
won't sit past its best in the fridge
and will be taken under the lime trees

so the bread will be fresher,
the grass always green
on this side of the hill

I'm moving in with you

so you can tease the hairs of my skin
like a soft-fingered breeze

I'm moving in with you

because you need no double negative
to make a positive

because I love your multitasking
as you kiss me on your way
to the recycling box
with a milkbottle, a jamjar
and a clean tin can in your arms

I'm moving in with you

because you're Miss Parallel Universe

because you welcome me
in my entirety

I'm moving in with you

so we'll make love
when the day of the week
has a *d* in it,

because you laughed so much in bed
that your ears were flooded with tears

I'm moving in with you

because a pair of jays came to your window
with their sapphire flash
and disreputable air
and the nuthatch and the green
and greater spotted woodpeckers,
and the foxes looked up

I'm moving in with you

so our offices will come
within hailing distance
but we'll keep our discipline

and because I can tell
from your carbonated glance
fresh as the experienced dawn
as we pass maturely on the stairs
that we'll have a bit of a bundance

I'm moving in with you

because of our proximate exuberance

so I can write another poem
on my knees
at your ironing board

because the blood
has cantered, raced and roared
and is coming round again
for another tender tussle

I'm moving in with you

so the days will turn over
on their back,
look at the ceiling,
and whistle.

World

If you were that fishing boat,
I'd be the sea with the fish in it.

If you were that sea,
I'd be a wind.

If you were the wind,
I'd be a meadow.

If you were a meadow,
I'd be the earth.

If you were the earth,
I'd be the geology.
I'd be the oolitic masses.

If you were the earth,
I'd be the sea,
sails on the sea,
wind on the meadow,
whirling the grasses,
making its passes,
one with you and me.

Padding back from a wintry bathroom

As I pad back in the half-light
from the wintry bathroom
I can see you've splayed out
in long, hidden spurs
beneath the quilt
across a frozen sea
of sheets to headlands
where I find your feet.
And when I point out
that you're taking up the bed,
you tell me drowsily that when I go,
you take up all the time and things —
skittering on the space-time continuum.

In the way you've opened out
contented over crumpled fields of sea-ice
there's this vulnerable generosity
I could reach down to take
and join with mine, the quality
of ease within me
that you introduced me to.
Informed with a simple gratitude
for desire, for your slow-breathing
angularity, my thoughts begin
to gather to a point already warmed.
Relieved of the nocturnal ache
of being fifty-eight,
the time's disarmed.

Listen

The wind drives in
a soft irregularity of rain
against the window,
across the Goldberg Variations.
Their weave comes alive:
in tune and in time we are,
side by side on the floor,
in the dark.

Discoveries

They pollarded the limes.
It was just before I moved in with you.
There was a wall of them
their backs to the hillside
and they locked our richness in,
blotting out the world
except for winter
and all we'd brought with us.
In the heat they made
living curtains for the bed,
and watched us.

Now their raw stumps are bowed
and arranged in attitudes
of possibility and victimhood,
bleeding the last
of the late summer's sap.
The barber-surgeons are in repose
in their afterfug of tea and fags
and Sun.   The limes remind me
of the barber's shop on Saturdays,
the rapid fire of the scissors
and the windfalls on the sheet
now turned to an unremitting white.
We all, the trees included,
all resisted the temptation
to get up and run —
or did I, once I could?

Me moving in.
I'm holding off the thought
that unconnected acts
have meaning for us
with this sweeping back of curtains
to reveal the crops and bellies
of the distant fields
offered to wind and sun and rain,

the edge of London
spilling into Kent.
I give up, lie back
frowning at the thought
of disappeared complexity —
the squirrels puzzled
since they lost the limbs they ran on
or was it — could it be? —
the puzzles that were squirreled,
some of them to be unearthed
their living bodies raised
in exposed amazement?
It's the complicated
force of resurrection:
so many woods, who,
who would have believed it
so many leaves grizzled
and gone the way of the world
to be reborn, enjoyed,
the joy put back in them,
unlocked. The room
with a view of it's enough
for one who struggled
not to make connection,
wires in each hand
that yearned and strained
to lock into a living current,
all for the not-so-childish fear
of a spark and conflagration.

The room with a view's a hide too
with an eye for where the rim
of a flat earth pours
into imagined thickets
under a sky that stirs and deals
a vitality that's random.

I remember when I needed
to permit myself a wilderness
and couldn't find the word
but then I stumbled
on the meaning of encouragement:
you gave me heart and heard.
In that liberated space
I climb against the dusk,
and at my back the iron bar
of a black ridge gains mass
silently: I hurry on the gradient
but can't catch up
with the November leavings,
all the sun's last gifts of turquoise,
lemon, their fleeting scrawls
all out of reach.

Head over heels, hand in glove,
abandoning belief
in the magic single bound
to freedom I relied on,
just for once at one with the hills
and human, I'm observed
by a collective noun:
an intelligence of love.

The spotted leaves of some marsh orchids

I surface in the afternoon
from somewhere far away
and intimate, walled in
by lime trees offering green
hearts that flicker at the glass
in thousands.   I am dulled
still from the place
we've met each other in,
that mood for being served
that comes with the confidence of both.
And next to me, you're off
remembering again
with your flowerbook, alert
enough to hold in sight
the shapes and hues of leaves
and blossoms from our week.
A difference in you
surfaces a moment, clear
as a roller from far out
I celebrate
as it washes over me:
your grasp of the particular,
what you see and I pass over,
needing to be shown
what's at my feet on my own land,
interrupted in the sweep
of clouds on my horizon.
I will glimpse a plant's complexity
if that - then it's gone again,
a fleeting stillness in the brush
while you are someone
with an eye that gathers,
who pursues, retains, resolves
and is resolved by this: and nurtures,
for all healing comes
from this precise desire.

I turn back to the leaves,
moved by the thought
that I might be seeing
the particularity itself
in another for the first time,
and I try to remember
nothing much:
the sea campion
asking for butterflies
on the cliffs.

In Sickness

1

As we drive west
through the winter solstice,
the lights blink at us
with their swift cold amber.

You are drawn and shrunk
with tiredness.   It's cellular,
your enemy, your illness,
it outnumbers you.

You need to understand
its grain and rhythm,
to observe, outwit,
and channel it.

We hurtle on towards
the valleys that have grown
to cup so much of us;
with stealth, we'll stalk

your shy absconded health;
together we will ease you up
from the cloudy riverbed
that calls you back, and walk.

2 *Chamber Music*

You set the resonance
of cherished wood
to mend the cell walls
that have blown down

in your puzzling interior storm.
It can't be done
with music that requires
energy it won't give back.

Which is a metaphor for us.
You find the room
for a generosity of mind
that overflows through what I see,

since like a drowning man
I found it in me
to insist on the surprising
value I put on my life

through you,
who'll be my wife.

River

Whatever the jostling,
confused intentions
that I harboured once
to have my way with you,
you feared the plaited river-ropes
of intimacy I proposed, and anyway,
I was unformed as water;
and the beauties in us
that we see now
needed to be shaped
with both our lifetimes.
We divided and the sandy bank
between us as we ran
became an island,
thickened, took our lives aground,
and grew trees, thickets, hearths
and London villages —
though with a city's substance
in, I insist, a division made of sand.
Provisional we ran; against all evidence
I knew I had the unifying river in me.
Currents that carried the seed
of memory of the other
past the continuing strand
as we wound on toward the unknown
shadowed water of the afternoon,
now we are together
and the weathered ropes of us
are twined, and roll and glisten
with a robust hope
that we still play thus
whenever the sea
may come for us.

To arrive at breakfast each
day with you
like a little boy at the beach

The mistake

These days above my brows
that beetle, there's a desert waste,
all skin and bone.
It's where the mistake arose:

a scaly crater,
crenellated pillbox
waiting for a long-spent war
that beached elsewhere,
a simple life-form
here to usher in the end of time,
my lizard crest.

Primitive relic, lovetest
crowing that it's cancerous,
redundant till it finds itself a home
and a lease of life
not unlike me, its host,
or mistletoe —
but boasting a distinguished name,
the Squamous Carcinoma:
the epitome of scaliness
that squats on my head
like a puffed-up toad
babbling of hats.
May be a mistake,
but it's no misnomer.

Here death gets to ride out in the park,
rides well, could just spawn deluded cults
but passes on like an asteroid
with a silent whoosh.

An alien unicorn.

A nipple on a hill.

It's easily removed
although, no fear,
it's giving me a masterclass
of living in the moment: the taker
laying down the law to the maker.

Child of climate change
and hairloss, so there's no wriggling
out of my responsibility for this.

Go on, whatever you call yourself,
humiliate the last residue
of youth that hung in there
like an old man to a moving train.

But I'm glad to be living here with you.

Gathering

You're all smiles, you're
loving uptake, gold-dust,
precious bones.   But most
of all you're a bowl
of strawberries, blueberries,

raspberries with their soft silent rasp,
and rich cold yoghurt:
you have that appetising integrity,
the presence, the clarity,
and how slowly savoured.

It was in the way
you arranged the flowers
I brought you, your hands
and your attention
and your pleasure at one.

Our past begins to gather up
in sprays, to shape into
an unguarded wood;
it's full of birdsong,
wealth more than enough.

The way they swirl
about the leaves,
it takes only two
to create a flurrying
cloud of goldfinches.

The Harrowing of the Squamous Cell Carcinoma

He's quiet as a handyman.
The surgeon's inner mind
is muttering in dialogue with steel.
It's just his implements.
From the blue-toilet-tissue-covered
workbench that will drink my fluids
like the good earth, I can visualise
his concentrated frown — and near to me
(where's me?) I hear the process
of engagement of his stout blades
through the thick worsted fabric of my flesh.
Who would have thought the old man
to have had so much meat on the bone
of the cranium?

Later I laughed, like a surgeon
freed from the terrain of hurt,
with my friends in a soft yellow light
over rare breed Ludlow chop,
purple-headed broccoli
and the flesh of the onion,
transparent, crisp
at the edge, well done,
and eight staples in a tiny henge
to hold the dressing on my crown
with the precarious effect
of balancing a fried egg on my head:
such hoots of laughter as to strain
the gleaming tent-pegs in my scalp
until the dressing crinkled and became a flower.
Who would have thought, so many muscles
in his scalp responding to the old man's moods
to make him a magician?
So much laughter, so much pain and dinner
and my dear friends offering to stroll down
for me to the stationer's, for a staple remover.

Another day, down to the Injuries Unit
for the plucking of the steel-edged flower,
the unveiling of the plug: if only the nurse
could have shortened her tight-lipped
pause at the sight of it.
The images mass on the border of my identity
to redefine with the invader's language,
oh, and to enrich: the first wave left
fittingly to my loyal love, in hard words
there's a hole in my head
that a golfball would fit comfortably in,
echoing the surgeon's sporting imprecision
that he took a divot, one I presume
he grubbed out with his niblick.

I'm developing my repertoire,
my banquet of unnatural events,
my gabbling cure:
hit by a meteorite,
disqualified from the seniors' egg-and-spoon
for sporting an illegal declivity;
a water-feature, a mental birdbath,
here's a man to be cast out in an open boat with
since the dew will have a small depression
to gather in; a facility
in the top of my head for the third eye —
something to keep an eye on the weather, sir? —
and out of the top of my head
comes one of those whooshing,
ectoplasmic beams of light
and all the kids shout
'Ghostbusters' when I walk into the room:
the moment that I wish could go on
to the crack of doom.

I'm running the gauntlet
of the nervous glance
in the crowded train.
Then the dialogue in the dark
with a malignant absence, a heady rumour

ready to make do and mend.
And to reach out for another glass of reserva,
the reserves of humour.
It's so neat and round.

I choose to fall back on my supernatural relief
and its potent special effects.
Through the top of my head
I observe the movement of the clouds,
a kind of integrated lighthouse-keeper
here on my daily constitutional
in the hanging gardens of Horniman.
There are consolations, powers
as you wait in the gathering silence
for the first drop that will bring the storm
as when you know the applause
will come for the singer.
Here the City's towers group
and gather their reports of gloom,
their backs to St.Paul's dome; they appear
to be deciding what to do with it.
Above them rolls the storm, slowly
in its melting anger of dark chocolate.
Against it, far off, there's a string
of sixty white birds
pointed to Scandinavia, pearls
that roll and rearrange themselves
on the steep damp fabric
of the breathing clouds.
In that distance I detect
the earth's curve beckoning,
and uplift, downdraught, reaper,
reckoning, the beautiful
receding opportunity:
the animate high silver things
that strike without resistance
for the north,
whatever may lie there
or be the truth
or the way through the literal light.

January

I had forgotten who I was.

It's all right, it comes back.

There'll be something stirring
under the snow:
the forgiving, the fullness,
the remembering.

I've learned to recall
myself alone.
Then somebody
slips in beside me.

Thursday, after making love

Footsteps and the rustle of clothes,
it's Thursday and her hair is drying
from drowned rat's tails
to electrified scarecrow woman
to presentable for the world.
The day's meandering
and you sink deeper under the quilt
and realise you have a smile
that's a mile deep
and it'll go about the day with you.
This is what would have been
if you'd dared imagine,
and it is.

Wedding video

It's obsolete technology,
the wedding video,
the way mirrors never will be
since they've always given you
a fair chance to compose yourself.
It's chastening to see yourself
unawares at your own wedding,
an ordinary man
with a strange hooting laugh
and grooves in his neck
that deepen like valleys in the evening,
deepen like his own happiness.

Five years of this illness pass

Stumped but not confounded
I resort to boiling calm
out of my protective rage.
After all my flighted
messages, I'm grounded.
It's where I am for you,
laid flat and taking in
the sky we fall to contemplate as one.
In parallel
we drink from the horizon,
deep in conversation as we do,
teasing out the paths
toward the energy that waits
beneath some mountain
we seem not to have the wherewithal
to recognise.
Every bush hides a practitioner
with the fragment of a score
torn from a place of certainty.
It's no game to choose
and fix and learn.
These are your precious
molecules we practise on,
the strewn harps
of your mitochondria unstrung.
Indoors, the cupboards of instruction
drift across the drowned floors.
Glance through the window
and you'll see the mythic cars
I've laid my hands on,
silver, ambered in the fog
lit by October lamps;
beside me all the winged sandals
I could ever gather that might fit.
All's set to take you
where you need to go.
Once we know.

Cave

I've pasted a little icon of us
where you click Start,
reduced so it's almost secret.
In it, we've been married
already for days.
Your eyes are minimised
behind your shades.
I wear a summer hat
that's now worn itself to shreds.
Electronic icons don't do that,
pristine till their spark goes out.
Beneath the summer hat,
behind the shades,
our eyes are a glint
stashed at the back of a cave
ready for when we need it.
The icon is a keyhole
torch into summer.

Life with you

Life with you's
an intimately strange,
familiar thing:
enjoyed in turn
by future selves and past,

durable and welcome
as the buoyancy
of turf in a wild place,
weathered,
replicated, subtly
transforming, will last.

Being strong

Having to be strong another year,
another hour, we must be ready
for the sudden glare of the opening door
of all the griefs. They break in
and there's no answering the wind
that will take our soul or strengthen it.
We have a limit, set
in the unbearable barchart of the soul.

We're tired of the endless
muscle-shift when the ground heaves,
the planet coming up to meet us
and withdrawing its favour,
the steadfastness and bend
of the way of the trees.
We listen for the many ends
of the tree in us, the note sustained

to a point in the wood, the gust
that will bend us nearly past resilience,
will have us creak and scream
but retrieve a shaken equilibrium,
breathing fast, bound with love.
What's new is you remake me
when I break. Along the line
of the mend I sense

the light feathering of trust.